MY LAST WISHES™
This is a Book about My Life.

It contains information about significant events that have taken place, some of which is already known. More importantly though it tells of who I love and have loved, what's had special meaning for me throughout my life, what I've enjoyed doing and who and what's made an impact on me. These are all things that I want my loved ones to know about, so that when the time comes for me to go, their burden will be lessened and their grief may be made a little easier to bear. They'll know how I would like to be remembered and what I'd like to be remembered for. These are My Last Wishes.

_____   _____
Name   Date

LAST WISHES™

Remembering the past...
Honouring the present...
Looking toward the future...

MY LAST WISHES™

I would like

NAME _____

to administer My Last Wishes,
and
then I would like this Book to be kept by

NAME _____

WITH THANKS FROM _____ DATED _____

My
LAST WISHES™

Remembering the past …
Honoring the present …
Looking toward the future …

Helen Read

BALBOA.
PRESS

A DIVISION OF HAY HOUSE

www.mylastwishesbook.com
enquiry@mylastwishesbook.com

Balboa Press books may be ordered through booksellers or by contacting:

Balboa Press
A Division of Hay House
1663 Liberty Drive
Bloomington, IN 47403
www.balboapress.com.au
1-(877) 407-4847

ISBN: 978-1-4525-0483-4 (sc)
ISBN: 978-1-4525-0484-1 (e)

Library of Congress Control Number: 2012906461

Because of the dynamic nature of the Internet, any web addresses or links contained in this book may have changed since publication and may no longer be valid. The views expressed in this work are solely those of the author and do not necessarily reflect the views of the publisher, and the publisher hereby disclaims any responsibility for them.

The information, ideas, and suggestions in this book are not intended to render legal advice. Before following any suggestions contained in this book, you should consult your personal attorney. Neither the author nor the publisher shall be liable or responsible for any loss or damage allegedly arising as a consequence of your use or application of any information or suggestions in this book.

Printed in the United States of America

Balboa Press rev. date: 04/18/2012

ACKNOWLEDGEMENTS

Thank you so much to my family and friends, who have given me
their wholehearted support and encouragement in this venture.
It's been invaluable.

And importantly, thank you very much for buying
and using this Book.
My hope is that it can truly help you and your family.

MY LAST WISHES has been written by Helen Read.
Inspiration came from experiences in her own family and through her work
as a Civil Celebrant. Her hope is that this book will help other families to unite
and leave them comforted in the knowledge that their loved one's wishes
were honoured and fulfilled.

What people are saying about this book:

"I have recently gone through a bereavement in the family and wanted to let you know
how grateful I was that my Dad had used your product. He wasn't expecting to die,
but he did plan for contingencies and had filled out a great number of the details
just in case. When he didn't make it out of hospital, it made planning the service
so simple, because we knew we were doing what HE wanted. Many thanks."

"I found My Last Wishes so easy to use and my family now has peace of mind."

"Mum wanted us to now her plans and where she kept things.
My Last Wishes not only made that possible but it's also given us
Mum's special memories to keep."

"Everyone needs to have a Will, a Power of Attorney and My Last Wishes.
I can see it solving a lot of family problems when I'm gone."

CONTENTS

INTRODUCTION

My Last Wishes has been designed not only to record milestones and memories in a very personal account of your life to date, but to assist loved ones who are left behind. In the face of grief it is they who have the difficult task of compiling information for a Priest, Celebrant, Minister, or Funeral Director and quite often important details are overlooked. Who better to tell your life story than yourself?

In the following pages you'll find stages of life covered by various headings. Some events will have already taken place in your life whilst others haven't yet unfolded. Not everything will apply to you, and you might prefer not to fill in some details at all, but you'll be able to pick and choose as to what you do record. In some instances you'll need to make a choice and strike out the alternative statement. There's a section where *financial information* can be passed on and there's also a *Family Health Record*, which can prove to be invaluable with regard to genetic conditions. In the event of a photographic presentation at your funeral or memorial service there is provision for you to nominate favourite *photos* that you'd like to have shown. Remember that **My Last Wishes** can be updated by you at any time simply by filling in new details on the *Update* pages at the end of each section. An annual update on your birthday would be an ideal way to record changes from the past year, whilst a new year of life stretches ahead of you.

It's completely up to you as to where you begin filling out the details for **My Last Wishes.** You may like to start at the beginning of the book and work your way through, or you may prefer to start with the *My Life* section. There's no set time as to how long this will take you either, as it's really dependent upon how much information you include. The section entitled *My Last Wishes for my Funeral* gives you the opportunity to plan your own funeral ceremony. There's also a *checklist* to go through which may be useful to your family when they need to contact various organisations on your behalf, together with an example of a letter that can be used for this purpose.

This is all about remembering the past, honouring the present and looking toward the future. Your loved ones will know exactly what your last wishes are and they won't be burdened spending weeks, or even months in some cases, tracking down information that's needed. Most importantly though, not only will you have peace of mind, but you'll also be leaving an everlasting legacy for your family to treasure.

Far from this being a sad activity, by confronting our mortality we tend to embrace life just that little bit tighter, which can be a truly enjoyable and liberating experience. You'll also hopefully discover more about yourself as you progress through this.

My Last Wishes is suitable for anyone of any age and it can be very rewarding for family members to complete it together. It may be the case that parents who are elderly need assistance from a son or daughter to write this, and thoughts or feelings you never knew they'd had will emerge.

Humour can be a great relief in times of sadness, so if there are funny anecdotes or jokes that have special meaning, don't hesitate to include them.

Finally, please make sure that someone close to you knows that you've completed **My Last Wishes** and keep it in a safe place. Tell them where it is, but also give them one of the *Location Cards* that are included in the back of this book. Please be aware that **My Last Wishes** is not a legal document and does not in any way replace a Last Will and Testament or a Power of Attorney.

HELEN READ, CMC

MY LAST WISHES FOR MY FUNERAL

I would like my funeral/memorial arrangements to be handled by
Relative's/Friend's Name _____.

He/she can be contacted on the following phone number at this address _____
_____
_____
_____
_____.

I have a preference for a Funeral Director. It is _____
_____
_____
_____
_____.

I do not have a preference for a Funeral Director.

I have prepaid $_____ of my Funeral expenses with _____
_____
_____
_____
_____.

I have Insurance to cover the cost of my Funeral with _____
_____
_____
_____
_____.

The paperwork for this is located _____
_____
_____.

I have made arrangements in my Will for my Funeral expenses to be paid for by my Estate.

I have not as yet made provision for my Funeral costs.

I will leave all decisions regarding the type of coffin/casket used to my Funeral Arranger.

I would like to have a standard/eco friendly/decorated/painted coffin.
/I would like a casket instead of a coffin.

I would like an open/closed coffin/casket at my Funeral Service.

I would like something special placed on my coffin/casket during the Service, namely _____
_____
_____
_____
_____.

I would then like this given to _____
_____.

I have no preference as to what I wear./I would like to be wearing _____
_____
_____
_____.

I have no preference as to what I take with me./I would like to have with me _____
_____
_____
_____.

I will let my family decide if they wish to view my body.

I do not wish to have my body viewed.

I would like the Service to be officiated by a Priest/Celebrant/Minister/Rabbi/Monk/as Specified,
namely _____.

from _____
_____.

and held at _____
_____
_____.

I have no preference as to who conducts my Funeral.

I have no preference as to where it is held.

I would like the following organisations/clubs to participate in my Funeral Service _____
_____
_____
_____
_____.

I would/would not like a Death and/or Funeral Notice advertised.

I would not like my age mentioned at my Funeral.

I don't mind if my age is mentioned during proceedings.

I would be pleased for my family, friends and acquaintances to be in attendance./I would like invited guests only to attend. (See attached list if required)

I would like a small Ceremony with just my immediate family present.

I would like a Requiem Mass.

I would like a Memorial Service for those who cannot attend my private Funeral.

I would like floral tributes. My favourite flowers are _____
_____
_____
_____
_____.

I would like donations to be made in lieu of floral tributes. I would like these donations made to

_____

_____

_____

_____

_____.

I would like doves/balloons/butterflies released.

I would like some other form of tribute/remembrance chosen by my Funeral Arranger.

If it's possible I would like an organist/soloist/band/piper to play.

I do not wish to have any music played.

I would like my Funeral Arranger to choose the music which is played.

I would like some of my favourite music played, namely _____

_____

_____

_____

_____

_____

_____

_____.

I have a favourite reading/poem which I would like read. It is _____

_____

_____

_____

_____

_____

_____

_____.

(See attached if required)

There are some events and circumstances that I would not like spoken about in my eulogy. (See attached if required)

I have written my own eulogy. (See attached if required)

I leave the writing of my Eulogy to my family and my friends.

I would like my husband/wife/son/daughter/brother/sister/father/mother/friend, _____
_____
to be asked to read my Eulogy. If this is too upsetting a task for them, then I would like the Priest/
Celebrant/Minister/Rabbi/Monk/to read it.

I would like my Eulogy read by the Priest/Celebrant/Minister/Rabbi/Monk.

I would like my cultural background to be observed during the Service.

I have nominated some photos that have special meaning to me and should there be a photographic
presentation I would like them used.

I will let my Funeral Arranger decide on the appropriateness of whether to photograph, video or
do a live webcast of my Funeral Service.

I would/would not like photos taken during my Funeral Service.

I would/would not like my Funeral Service videoed.

I would/would not like a live webcast of my Funeral Service for those who cannot attend.

I would like pallbearers to be the Funeral Director's staff.

I would like the following people asked to be pallbearers _____
_____
_____
_____
_____.

I will leave the choice of pallbearers to my Funeral Arranger.

I would like to be buried. If it's possible, I would like to be buried at _____
_____
_____
_____
_____.

I would like an additional small Service at the graveside.

I do not wish to have an additional Service at the graveside.

I have made no arrangements for a burial plot or crematorium resting place./I have pre purchased my final resting place at _____
_____.

I will leave the choice of a monument/plaque/headstone and the wording to my Family.

If it's possible, I would specifically like _____
_____
_____
_____.

I would like a monument/plaque/headstone to read _____
_____
_____
_____.

Special Instructions _____
_____
_____
_____
_____
_____.

I would like to be cremated. If it's possible, I would like my ashes _____
_____
_____
_____.

I do not wish to have a memorial plaque.

I would like a memorial plaque at the Crematorium to read _____
_____
_____
_____.

Special instructions _____
_____
_____

_____

_____.

I would like family and friends who've attended my Funeral to have an opportunity to gather together for light refreshments afterwards.

If it's possible, I would like my wake to be held at _____

_____

_____

_____.

I would prefer that there is no wake.

A concern that I have regarding my Funeral is _____

_____

_____

_____

_____

_____

_____

_____

_____

_____.

I do not wish to be buried or cremated. Instead I would like to _____

_____

_____

_____

_____.

If I should die overseas, I would like my remains to be _____

_____

_____

_____

_____.

Alternative arrangements

_____

_____

_____

_____

_____

_____

_____

_____

_____

_____

_____

_____

_____

_____

_____

_____

_____

_____

_____

_____

_____

_____

_____

_____

_____

_____

_____

_____

_____

_____

_____

_____

_____

_____

_____

_____

_____

_____.

HELEN READ

Listed below are family members to be notified.

Name _____
Phone _____
Email _____
Address _____

Name _____
Phone _____
Email _____
Address _____

Name _____
Phone _____
Email _____
Address _____

Name _____
Phone _____
Email _____
Address _____

Name _____
Phone _____
Email _____
Address _____

Name _____
Phone _____
Email _____
Address _____

Name _____
Phone _____
Email _____
Address _____

Name _____

Phone _____

Email _____

Address _____

Name _____

Phone _____

Email _____

Address _____

Name _____

Phone _____

Email _____

Address _____

Name _____

Phone _____

Email _____

Address _____

I would like these friends and associates notified please.

Name _____

Phone _____

Email _____

Relationship _____

Name _____

Phone _____

Email _____

Relationship _____

Name _____

Phone _____

Email _____

Relationship _____

Name   _____

Phone   _____

Email   _____

Relationship   _____

Name   _____

Phone   _____

Email   _____

Relationship   _____

Name   _____

Phone   _____

Email   _____

Relationship   _____

Name   _____

Phone   _____

Email   _____

Relationship   _____

Name   _____

Phone   _____

Email   _____

Relationship   _____

Name   _____

Phone   _____

Email   _____

Relationship   _____

Name   _____

Phone   _____

Email   _____

Relationship   _____

Additional family members to be notified

_____
_____
_____
_____
_____
_____
_____
_____
_____
_____
_____
_____
_____
_____
_____
_____
_____
_____
_____
_____
_____
_____
_____
_____
_____
_____
_____
_____
_____
_____
_____
_____
_____
_____
_____.

Additional friends and associates to be notified

_____
_____
_____
_____
_____
_____
_____
_____
_____
_____
_____
_____
_____
_____
_____
_____
_____
_____
_____
_____
_____
_____
_____
_____
_____
_____
_____
_____
_____
_____
_____
_____
_____
_____
_____
_____

Additional Information

_____

_____

_____

_____

_____

_____

_____

_____

_____

_____

_____

_____

_____

_____

_____

_____

_____

_____

_____

_____

_____

_____

_____

_____

_____

_____

_____

_____

_____

_____

_____

_____

_____

_____

_____

_____

_____.

Updates to My Last Wishes for my Funeral

_____

_____

_____

_____

_____

_____

_____

_____

_____

_____

_____

_____

_____

_____

_____

_____

_____

_____

_____

_____

_____

_____

_____

_____

_____

_____

_____

_____

_____

_____

_____

_____

_____

_____

_____

_____

_____

CHECKLIST FOR MY FAMILY

The relevant people, organisations and businesses listed below will need to be advised as soon as possible. Some of them may require a copy of the death certificate before they can proceed to alter their records.

Foreign Pension authority
Solicitor/Barrister/Lawyer/Attorney or Public Trustee
Executor of Will
Place of Work/Employer
Business Associates
Doctor—GP
Doctor—Specialists
Medical authority
Pharmacist
Ambulance Service
Specialists
Hospitals
Home Nursing Service
Social Worker
Health Insurance
Home Help
Dentist
Physiotherapist/Optometrist
Volunteering organisations
Home Delivery Services
Church/Religious organisation
Community organisations
Service organisations
Clubs
Veterans' Group
Ex-service Association
Employee Association
Trade Union
Professional Associations
Banks

Building Societies
Credit Unions
Friendly Society
Credit Card Providers
Finance Companies
Accountant
Taxation/Revenue Office
Insurance Companies
Superannuation Funds
Electricity/Gas/Telephone
Local Government
Electoral Office
Home Appliance Rental Company
Landlord
Garden/Mower Service
Transport—Licence and vehicle registration
Postal Service

Additional information

Counselling Services.

- The American Academy of Grief Counselling
- ADEC, The Thanatology Association
- American Counselling Association

There are some organisations that will require notification in writing either from a family member or from the Executor and the following example may be of help in this situation.

Name and address of organisation
Date

To Whom it may Concern

This is to advise you of the death of _____ FULL NAME
of _____ ADDRESS
_____ POSTAL/ZIP CODE _____ STATE, *on* _____DATE
It is my understanding that he/she dealt with your organisation and the relevant membership/reference number I have is _____.

If required, I can be contacted at _____ ADDRESS
or by phoning _____ PHONE NUMBER. *My relationship to the deceased is that of*_____.

Thank you for your prompt attention to this matter.

Yours sincerely,

_____ SIGNATURE
_____ PRINT YOUR NAME

MY FINANCES

I have accounts at the following Banks/Building Societies/Credit Unions

Bank	_____	Bank	_____
Branch	_____	Branch	_____
BSB	_____	BSB	_____
Account #	_____	Account #	_____
Building Society	_____	Credit Union	_____
Branch	_____	Branch	_____
BSB	_____	BSB	_____
Account #	_____	Account #	_____

You will find additional details regarding these accounts

_____

_____

_____

_____

_____.

I have Loans (Car/Mortgage/Retail Stores/Other) with

Car	_____
Mortgage	_____
Retail Store	_____
Retail Store	_____
Retail Store	_____
Retail Store	_____

You will find relevant paperwork for the above

_____.

Other _____

Other _____

Other _____

Other _____

I have the following Credit Cards

Card _____ Account # _____

Card _____ Account # _____

Card _____ Account # _____

Card _____ Account # _____

Card _____ Account # _____

Card _____ Account # _____

Card _____ Account # _____

Card _____ Account # _____

Card _____ Account # _____

Card _____ Account # _____

Additional information is located _____

_____

_____.

I have Insurances (Health/Life/Home/Contents/Car/Other) with

Company _____ Phone _____

Type of Insurance _____

Policy Number/s _____

Paid Every _____ Amount Paid _____

Company _____ Phone _____

Type of Insurance _____

Policy Number/s _____

Paid Every _____ Amount Paid _____

Company   _____ Phone _____

Type of Insurance _____

Policy Number/s _____

Paid Every   _____ Amount Paid _____

Company   _____ Phone _____

Type of Insurance _____

Policy Number/s _____

Paid Every   _____ Amount Paid _____

Company   _____ Phone _____

Type of Insurance _____

Policy Number/s _____

Paid Every   _____ Amount Paid _____

Company   _____ Phone _____

Type of Insurance _____

Policy Number/s _____

Paid Every   _____ Amount Paid _____

Company   _____ Phone _____

Type of Insurance _____

Policy Number/s _____

Paid Every   _____ Amount Paid _____

I have Superannuation with the following Company/Companies

Company   _____ Phone _____

Policy Number _____

Company _____ Phone _____

Policy Number _____

Company _____ Phone _____

Policy Number _____

Additional information regarding Superannuation is located_____

_____

_____

_____

_____

_____.

I do not receive a pension./I receive a pension from _____

_____

_____

_____.

My customer number is _____.

I do not receive an allowance./I receive an allowance from _____

_____

_____

_____.

I have a Share Broker. His/her name and contact details are _____

_____

_____

_____

_____.

I have a share portfolio, the details of which are _____

_____

_____

_____

_____

_____

_____

_____.

I manage my own share portfolio.

I own property (owned outright or mortgaged/singly or jointly) at _____
_____
_____
_____
_____
_____.

I rent the property I live in from _____
_____
_____
_____.

I do not have/I have a Safe/Safety Deposit Box. The key/pin number is kept _____
_____
_____
_____.

And the Safe/Box is located in/at _____
_____
_____
_____.

I have hidden things that are precious to me under/in _____
_____
_____
_____.

Other Investments _____
_____
_____
_____
_____
_____
_____
_____
_____.

I do not have/I have an Accountant. His/her contact details are _____

_____

_____

_____.

I do my own taxation returns./I have my taxation returns done by _____

_____

_____

_____.

My Taxation Number is _____.

I do not have/I have a Financial Advisor/Planner. His/her contact details are _____

_____

_____

_____.

I do not have/I have a Solicitor. His/her contact details are _____

_____

_____

_____.

I have made a Last Will and Testament. It is kept _____

_____

_____

_____.

My Executor is/Executors are _____

_____

_____

_____.

and the contact details are _____

_____

_____

_____.

I do not have a Last Will and Testament.

I have made provision for Guardianship of my child/children in my Last Will and Testament.

I have made no provision for Guardianship of my child/children in my Last Will and Testament, but in the event that they are left alone I would like them to spend time with _____

_____

_____

_____.

Guardianship of my child/children is not applicable.

If it's possible, I would like my pets taken care of by _____

_____

_____

_____.

I have completed a Power of Attorney document. The person appointed is _____

_____

_____

_____.

And the contact details are _____

_____

_____

_____.

This document is kept _____

_____

_____

_____.

I have not appointed a Power of Attorney.

My personal papers (birth certificate, marriage certificate, passport etc) are kept _____

_____

_____

_____.

Items loaned by me to family/friends that are to be returned include _____

_____

_____

_____

_____.

Items that I have already given away to family/friends that are to be kept by them include _____

_____

_____

_____

_____

_____

_____.

Valuable items in my possession which could be overlooked are _____

_____

_____

_____

_____

_____

_____.

Passwords that may be needed for various computer applications, mobile phone access etc.

Item _____ Password _____

Item _____ Password _____

Item _____ Password _____

Item _____ Password _____

Item _____ Password _____

Item _____ Password _____

Item _____ Password _____

Item _____ Password _____

Item _____ Password _____

I do not have a post office box. I have a post office box. It is at _____

_____

_____

_____.

The number is   and the key is located _____.

I own a Company/various Companies, namely _____

_____

_____

_____

_____

_____

_____.

I am in partnership in a Company/various Companies, namely _____

_____

_____

_____

_____

_____

_____.

I am a Director on the Board of _____

_____

_____

_____

_____

_____

_____.

Other business interests include _____

_____

_____

_____

_____

_____

_____.

I volunteer my time and services to _____

_____

_____

_____

_____

_____

_____.

Additional Share Portfolio information

_____

Additional information regarding Property

_____
_____
_____
_____
_____
_____
_____
_____
_____
_____
_____
_____
_____
_____
_____
_____
_____
_____
_____
_____
_____
_____
_____
_____
_____
_____
_____
_____
_____
_____
_____
_____
_____
_____
_____
_____
_____
_____.

Additional information regarding Other Investments

_____

_____

_____

_____

_____

_____

_____

_____

_____

_____

_____

_____

_____

_____

_____

_____

_____

_____

_____

_____

_____

_____

_____

_____

_____

_____

_____

_____

_____

_____

_____

_____

_____

_____

_____

_____

_____.

Additional information regarding My Finances

_____

_____

_____

_____

_____

_____

_____

_____

_____

_____

_____

_____

_____

_____

_____

_____

_____

_____

_____

_____

_____

_____

_____

_____

_____

_____

_____

_____

_____

_____

_____

_____

_____

_____

Additional information regarding My Finances

_____
_____
_____
_____
_____
_____
_____
_____
_____
_____
_____
_____
_____
_____
_____
_____
_____
_____
_____
_____
_____
_____
_____
_____
_____
_____
_____
_____
_____
_____
_____
_____
_____
_____
_____
_____
_____.

Updates to My Finances

Updates to My Finances

_____

_____

_____

_____

_____

_____

_____

_____

_____

_____

_____

_____

_____

_____

_____

_____

_____

_____

_____

_____

_____

_____

_____

_____

_____

_____

_____

_____

_____

_____

_____

_____

_____

_____.

Updates to My Finances

_____

_____

_____

_____

_____

_____

_____

_____

_____

_____

_____

_____

_____

_____

_____

_____

_____

_____

_____

_____

_____

_____

_____

_____

_____

_____

_____

_____

_____

_____

_____

_____

_____

_____

_____

MY FAMILY HEALTH RECORD

My Doctor's name is _____
_____
_____.

He/she is located at _____
_____
_____.

My Specialist's name is _____
_____
_____.

He/she is located at _____
_____
_____.

My Medical number is _____.

I do not have/I have health insurance. My Fund is _____
_____
and my membership number is _____.

I do not have any health information concerning my Mother.

My Mother had/has the following health issues _____
_____
_____.

My Mother smoked/never smoked/smokes./My Mother was a smoker but gave up in/when ____
_____
_____.

She died in (Date) _____ aged _____ from _____
_____
_____.

My Mother's parents' health was _____
_____
_____.

My Mother's mother died in (Date) _____ aged _____ from_____
_____
_____.

My Mother's father died in (Date) _____ aged _____ from _____
_____
_____.

I do not have any health information concerning my Father.

My Father has/had the following health issues _____
_____
_____.

My Father smoked/never smoked/smokes./My Father was a smoker but gave up in/when _____
_____
_____.

He died in (Date) _____ aged _____ from _____
_____
_____.

My Father's parents' health was _____
_____
_____.

My Father's mother died in (Date) _____ aged _____ from _____
_____
_____.

My Father's father died in (Date) _____ aged _____ from _____

_____

_____ .

Health problems encountered by my Uncles/Aunts include _____

_____

_____

_____

_____

_____ .

My Uncles/Aunts have had no major health problems.

Health problems encountered by my Brothers/Sisters include _____

_____

_____

_____

_____

_____ .

My Brothers/Sisters have had no major health problems.

Other close relatives of mine have had the following health issues _____

_____

_____

_____

_____

_____ .

I have always enjoyed good health.

I have no allergies.
I am allergic to _____

_____

_____

_____

_____ .

I have never smoked./I am a Smoker.

I gave up smoking in (Date) _____ after _____ years of smoking.

I have never been addicted to any substance./I have been addicted to _____

_____

_____

_____

_____

_____

_____.

Conditions I am currently being treated for include _____

_____

_____

_____

_____

_____

_____.

I have had a nagging problem with _____

_____

_____

_____

_____

_____

_____.

I have had health issues to do with _____

_____

_____

_____

_____

_____

_____

_____

_____

_____

_____

_____.

I have never had an operation. I have never been hospitalised.

I have had the following operations _____
_____
_____
_____
_____
_____
_____.

I have been an inpatient in these Hospitals _____
_____
_____
_____
_____
_____
_____.

I have implants and they are _____
_____
_____
_____
_____
_____
_____.

My Blood Group is _____./I do not know my Blood Group.

I am a Registered Organ Donor./I do not wish to donate my organs.

I have not registered as an organ donor but I would like to donate my organs.

I have made an Advanced Health Directive and it is located _____
_____
_____
_____.

I have not made an Advanced Health Directive.

Additional Information

_____

_____

_____

_____

_____

_____

_____

_____

_____

_____

_____

_____

_____

_____

_____

_____

_____

_____

_____

_____

_____

_____

_____

_____

_____

_____

_____

_____

_____

_____

_____

_____

_____

Updates to My Family Health Record

_____
_____
_____
_____
_____
_____
_____
_____
_____
_____
_____
_____
_____
_____
_____
_____
_____
_____
_____
_____
_____
_____
_____
_____
_____
_____
_____
_____
_____
_____
_____
_____
_____
_____
_____
_____
_____
_____
_____

Updates to My Family Health Record

_____
_____
_____
_____
_____
_____
_____
_____
_____
_____
_____
_____
_____
_____
_____
_____
_____
_____
_____
_____
_____
_____
_____
_____
_____
_____
_____
_____
_____
_____
_____
_____
_____
_____
_____
_____
_____
_____
_____
_____

Updates to My Family Health Record

_____
_____
_____
_____
_____
_____
_____
_____
_____
_____
_____
_____
_____
_____
_____
_____
_____
_____
_____
_____
_____
_____
_____
_____
_____
_____
_____
_____
_____
_____
_____
_____
_____
_____
_____
_____
_____
_____
_____.

MY LIFE

I was born on (Date) _____ at
_____ .

The date I arrived in this country was (Date) _____ .
I travelled with _____
I/We came on a _____
From _____
_____ .

My full name is _____
_____ .

Nicknames I've had include _____ .

Because _____
_____ .

My parents' names were _____
and _____ .

My Mother was born on (Date) _____ at
_____ .

She is still alive/She died on (Date) _____ at
_____ .

Her maiden name was _____
_____ .

Her occupation is/was _____
_____
_____ .

My Father was born on (Date) _____ at
_____.

He is still alive/He died on (Date) _____ at
_____.

His occupation is/was _____
_____
_____.

My parents did not marry./My parents married on (Date) _____ at
_____.

My Brothers and Sisters names, dates of birth and places of birth are _____
_____
_____
_____
_____
_____.

I am an only child.

My Stepmother's name is/was _____
_____.

She died on (Date) _____ at
_____.

She married my Father on (Date) _____ at
_____.

Her occupation is/was _____
_____
_____.

My Stepfather's name is/was _____
_____.

He died on (Date) _____ at
_____.

He married my Mother on (Date) _____ at
_____.

My parents were not/were religious and brought me up accordingly.

We attended services at _____
_____
_____.

My early life as a young child was _____
_____
_____
_____
_____
_____.

When I was young I remember playing _____
_____
_____.

I was always interested in _____
_____
_____.

We had pets, and they were _____
_____
_____
_____
_____.

Other animals we had were _____
_____
_____.

We never had a pet because _____
_____
_____
_____
_____.

We lived at _____

_____

_____

_____

_____.

When I was (Age) _____ we moved to

_____

_____

_____.

We also lived at _____

_____

_____

_____

_____.

Christmases and special occasions were spent with _____

_____

_____

_____

_____.

At _____

_____

_____

_____

_____

_____

_____

_____

_____

_____

_____

_____

_____

_____

_____

_____.

I attended Elementary/Primary School at _____
_____
_____
_____
_____
_____.

A friend from that time was _____
_____
_____
_____.

Memories include _____
_____
_____
_____
_____
_____
_____
_____
_____
_____
_____
_____.

I remember that I wanted to be _____
_____
_____
_____ when I grew up.

Family holidays were spent at _____
_____
_____
_____
_____.

I attended High/Secondary School at _____
_____
_____
_____
_____.

A friend from that time was _____
_____
_____.

Memories include

_____
_____
_____
_____
_____
_____
_____
_____
_____
_____
_____
_____
_____
_____.

I remember that I wanted to be _____
_____
_____ when I left school.

I liked school./I didn't enjoy school.

I was popular./I was bullied/made fun of.

People that made an impact on me during my school life were _____
_____
_____
_____
_____
_____
_____
_____
_____.

I finished school in (Date) _____ when I was (Age) _____.

I went on to study _____

_____

_____

_____

_____.

At

_____

_____

_____.

I worked part time from the age of _____ at/for _____

_____

_____

_____

_____.

I got a full time job when I left school working for _____

_____

_____

_____

_____.

My friends from this time were _____

_____

_____

_____.

A memorable Birthday from this time was when I turned (Age) _____.

I remember it because

_____

_____

_____

_____

_____

_____

_____.

I lived at home until I was _____
_____
_____.

I moved out of home and lived at/with _____
_____
_____.

To get around I used to walk/bicycle/get a lift/catch public transport or _____
_____
_____.

I used my parents' car and it was a _____
_____
_____.

I had my own car/motorbike. It was a _____
_____
_____.

And it cost me _____.

I had it for (Number of Weeks, Months, Years) _____.

The longest drive I took was to _____.

The first time I went on a plane was _____
_____
_____.

My first trip overseas was in (Date) _____ to

_____
_____.

When I graduated, my first career position was with _____
_____
_____
_____
_____
_____.

I have never been in the Services./I have served in the (Army/Air Force/Navy)

_____.

I went on to work for _____

_____

_____

_____.

I started my own business in (Date) _____.
I called it (Name) _____.

And I worked as a/an _____.

I went into partnership in (Date) _____ with

_____.

We called the business (Name) _____.

And we (Type of Business—eg made, sold)

_____

_____

_____.

The thing I really enjoyed about my work was _____

_____

_____

_____.

I didn't enjoy _____

_____

_____.

I regret that I didn't _____

_____

_____

_____

_____

_____.

Other things I've done in my working life include _____
_____
_____
_____
_____.

The highlight of my working life has been _____
_____
_____
_____
_____.

People who inspired me and helped me along the way during my career include _____
_____
_____
_____
_____.

My first love was _____
_____.

We met at _____
_____
_____
_____.

We used to go to _____
_____
_____
_____.

Other significant relationships in my life have included _____
_____
_____
_____
_____
_____
_____
_____.

I've never married because _____
_____
_____.

I met my future husband/wife when I was (Age) _____ in (Date) _____.

We met at _____
_____.

I was attracted by _____
_____
_____.

We used to go to _____
_____
_____.

His/her occupation was _____
_____
_____.

I became engaged to (Name) _____ when I was (Age) _____.

My parents approved/disapproved.

His/her parents approved/disapproved.

He/she lived at _____
_____
_____.

We married on (Date) _____ at
_____
_____.

Our wedding was _____
_____
_____
_____
_____

_____

_____

_____

_____

_____

_____

_____

_____.

We spent our honeymoon _____

_____

_____

_____

_____.

We didn't have a honeymoon.

Our first home was at _____

_____

_____.

We lived there for (Number of) _____ years.

We then moved to _____

_____

_____.

Other homes have included _____

_____

_____

_____

_____

_____

_____

_____

_____

_____.

The home I was happiest in was _____

_____

_____.

Because _____

_____

_____.

Our first child was born on (Date) _____ at

_____

_____.

His/her name is _____.

My other children's names, dates of birth and places of birth are

_____.

_____.

_____.

_____.

_____.

_____.

_____.

_____.

Why we/I chose the names we/I did for our children

_____

_____

_____

_____

_____

_____.

Additional information _____

_____

_____

_____

_____

_____

_____

_____.

A child/Children put into foster care/adopted out, and the reason why.

_____
_____
_____
_____
_____
_____
_____.

I've never had children because _____
_____
_____
_____
_____
_____
_____.

Our family life is/was best summed up as being _____
_____
_____
_____
_____
_____
_____.

My husband/wife is still alive/died on (Date) _____ at _____
_____.

My husband/wife and I separated/divorced in (Date) _____ because _____
_____
_____
_____
_____
_____
_____
_____
_____
_____
_____.

Other marriages/partnerships of mine were _____
_____
_____
_____
_____
_____
_____
_____.

In my life I've always valued _____
_____
_____
_____
_____
_____
_____.

I've tried to live by the principle of _____
_____
_____
_____
_____
_____
_____.

I believe in _____
_____
_____
_____
_____
_____
_____.

My favourite saying has been _____
_____
_____
_____
_____
_____.

Causes that I've followed and supported include _____
_____
_____
_____
_____
_____.

Community Service activities I've been involved in are _____
_____
_____
_____
_____
_____.

I've belonged to various organisations/clubs, including _____
_____
_____
_____
_____
_____.

My political ideals and beliefs are best summed up as _____
_____
_____
_____
_____
_____.

People have always said that I'm _____
_____
_____
_____
_____
_____.

I think I'm _____
_____
_____
_____
_____.

My personality is probably best described as _____
_____
_____
_____
_____
_____.

My most marked characteristics are _____
_____
_____
_____
_____
_____.

Things I find funny are _____
_____
_____
_____
_____
_____.

Things that make me sad include _____
_____
_____
_____
_____
_____.

I'm proud of _____
_____
_____
_____
_____
_____.

I've always been afraid of _____
_____
_____
_____
_____.

I wish I wasn't so _____

_____

_____

_____

_____

_____.

I've never liked my _____

_____

_____.

I wish I hadn't had _____

_____

_____.

I wish I could be more _____

_____

_____.

I wish other people would be more _____

_____

_____.

I wish I'd spent more time _____

_____

_____

_____

_____.

I always wanted to meet _____

_____

_____.

There was someone that I was thrilled to meet and this is how it happened.

_____

_____

_____

_____

_____

_____

_____

_____.

I wish I hadn't lost touch with _____

_____

_____.

I've always admired _____

_____

_____.

I always wanted to travel to _____

_____

_____.

I always wanted to live in _____

_____

_____.

My most treasured possession is my _____

_____

_____.

Something I always wanted to own was a _____

_____

_____.

I've liked/loved dancing./I don't like to dance.

_____

_____.

I've liked/loved singing./I've never liked my singing voice.

_____

_____.

I've always enjoyed _____

_____

_____

_____.

A thing of beauty to me is _____
_____
_____
_____
_____.

I'm very grateful for _____
_____
_____
_____
_____.

A favourite book is _____
_____
_____
_____.

A favourite writer is _____
_____
_____
_____.

A favourite movie is _____
_____
_____
_____.

A favourite television program is _____
_____
_____
_____.

A favourite actor/musician is _____
_____
_____.

A favourite piece of poetry was written by _____

_____

_____

_____.

And is called _____

_____

_____

_____.

When I listen to the radio, I listen to _____

_____

_____

_____.

I wish I'd learned to _____

_____

_____

_____

_____

_____.

I wish I'd been good at _____

_____

_____

_____

_____

_____.

A personal achievement that I'm proudest of is _____

_____

_____

_____

_____

_____.

Lifelong friends include _____

_____

_____

_____.

Great friends from recent years include _____

_____

_____

_____.

I've liked spending time with _____

_____

_____

_____.

I've always been able to rely on _____

_____

_____

_____.

The best period of my life has been _____

_____

_____

_____

_____

_____

_____

_____

_____

_____

_____

_____

_____

_____

_____.

The worst period of my life has been _____

_____

_____

_____

_____

_____

_____

_____
_____
_____
_____
_____
_____
_____
_____
_____
_____.

Challenges in life that I've had to face up to have included _____
_____
_____
_____
_____
_____
_____
_____
_____.

The deaths of family and friends that have really made an impact on me were those of _____
_____
_____
_____
_____
_____
_____
_____
_____.

Something that I have learned from life so far is _____
_____
_____
_____
_____
_____
_____.

The legacy I would like to leave behind is _____

_____

_____

_____

_____

_____

_____

_____

_____.

When I'm remembered I'd like to be thought of as someone _____

_____

_____

_____

_____

_____

_____

_____

_____

_____.

One last thing to say about …..

_____

_____

_____

_____

_____

_____

_____

_____

_____

_____

_____

_____

_____

_____.

What my faith means to me (continued)

_____
_____
_____
_____
_____
_____
_____
_____
_____
_____
_____
_____
_____
_____
_____
_____
_____
_____
_____
_____
_____
_____
_____
_____
_____
_____
_____
_____
_____
_____
_____
_____
_____
_____
_____.

My early life as a young child was (continued)

_____
_____
_____
_____
_____
_____
_____
_____
_____
_____
_____
_____
_____
_____
_____
_____
_____
_____
_____
_____
_____
_____
_____
_____
_____
_____
_____
_____
_____
_____
_____
_____
_____
_____.

Service history (continued)

_____
_____
_____
_____
_____
_____
_____
_____
_____
_____
_____
_____
_____
_____
_____
_____
_____
_____
_____
_____
_____
_____
_____
_____
_____
_____
_____
_____
_____
_____
_____
_____
_____
_____
_____
_____
_____.

Additional information on children put into foster care/adopted out (continued)

_____
_____
_____
_____
_____
_____
_____
_____
_____
_____
_____
_____
_____
_____
_____
_____
_____
_____
_____
_____
_____
_____
_____
_____
_____
_____
_____
_____
_____
_____
_____
_____
_____
_____
_____
_____.

The best period of my life has been (continued)

_____
_____
_____
_____
_____
_____
_____
_____
_____
_____
_____
_____
_____
_____
_____
_____
_____
_____
_____
_____
_____
_____
_____
_____
_____
_____
_____
_____
_____
_____
_____
_____
_____
_____.

The worst period of my life has been (continued)

_____

_____

_____

_____

_____

_____

_____

_____

_____

_____

_____

_____

_____

_____

_____

_____

_____

_____

_____

_____

_____

_____

_____

_____

_____

_____

_____

_____

_____

_____

_____

_____

_____.

Special Memories

_____
_____
_____
_____
_____
_____
_____
_____
_____
_____
_____
_____
_____
_____
_____
_____
_____
_____
_____
_____
_____
_____
_____
_____
_____
_____
_____
_____
_____
_____
_____
_____
_____
_____
_____
_____
_____
_____.

Special Memories

Special Memories

_____
_____
_____
_____
_____
_____
_____
_____
_____
_____
_____
_____
_____
_____
_____
_____
_____
_____
_____
_____
_____
_____
_____
_____
_____
_____
_____
_____
_____
_____
_____
_____
_____
_____
_____

Updates to My Life

_____

_____

_____

_____

_____

_____

_____

_____

_____

_____

_____

_____

_____

_____

_____

_____

_____

_____

_____

_____

_____

_____

_____

_____

_____

_____

_____

_____

_____

_____

_____

_____

_____.

Updates to My Life

_____

_____

_____

_____

_____

_____

_____

_____

_____

_____

_____

_____

_____

_____

_____

_____

_____

_____

_____

_____

_____

_____

_____

_____

_____

_____

_____

_____

_____

_____

_____

_____

_____

_____

_____

_____

_____

_____

_____

PHOTOGRAPHS I LIKE

Photo of _____.

Photo of _____.

Photo of _____.

Photo of _____.

Photo of _____.

Photo of _____.

Photo of _____.

Photo of _____.

Photo of _____.

Photo of _____.

Photo of _____.

Photo of _____.

Photo of _____.

Photo of _____.

Photo of _____.

Photo of _____.

These are location cards for **My Last Wishes**. When you've completed the book, and you've decided who you'd like to administer your last wishes, you'll need to let that person know where to locate it, e.g., top drawer of the filing cabinet in the study etc. Cut along the dotted lines below to make an individual card, fill in the location details, fold it, laminate it and give them the card. Additional cards are provided for changes in circumstances.

MY LAST WISHES™
A Book about My Life for my Family
Written by
It is located

www.mylastwishes.com.au

MY LAST WISHES™
A Book about My Life for my Family
Written by
It is located

www.mylastwishes.com.au

MY LAST WISHES™
A Book about My Life for my Family
Written by
It is located

www.mylastwishes.com.au

MY LAST WISHES™
A Book about My Life for my Family
Written by
It is located

www.mylastwishes.com.au